Astronomy

Rachel Firth

Designed by Lucy Owen

Consultant: Stuart Atkinson
Illustrated by John Woodcock
Edited by Jane Chisholm and Gillian Doherty

The Parkes Radio
Telescope in Australia

Contents

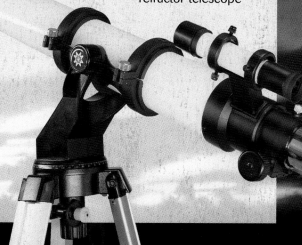

Internet links

Look for the Internet links boxes throughout this book. They contain descriptions of websites where you can find out more about astronomy. For links to these websites, go to **www.usborne-quicklinks.com** and type in the keywords "discovery astronomy".

★ Next to some of the pictures in this book you will see a star symbol. Wherever you see one of these, it means that you can download the picture from the **Usborne Quicklinks Website**. For more information on using the Internet, and downloading Usborne pictures, see inside the back cover.

Cover pictures: The Eagle Nebula, Mars, Neptune and Saturn
Title page: The Milky Way

A 100mm (4 inch) refractor telescope

Night sky ....

On a clear night, you can see thousands of stars in the sky. But what you see is just a tiny part of what's out in space. As well as stars, there are planets, moons, clouds of gas and huge stretches of empty space.

Measuring space

Distances between most things in space are so huge that it's difficult to imagine them. Scientists measure space distances in light years. One light year is 9.46 million million km (5.8 million million* miles), which is the distance light travels in a year.

Bright stars

Stars look like tiny bright lights in the night sky. They are huge balls of incredibly hot gas. But they look tiny because they are very, very far away. The Sun is our nearest star. There are billions of other stars like it scattered through space, varying in size and brightness.

* US = trillion

This is a group of stars known as the Pleiades. It contains about 500 stars. It's also known as the Seven Sisters because, on a clear night, you can see the seven brightest stars in the group with the naked eye.

Galaxies

Stars exist in enormous groups called galaxies, which are made up of billions of stars. You can see many galaxies with a powerful telescope, although some are too far away to see clearly.

Planets and moons

Planets are balls of rock or gas that move around, or orbit, a star. Earth is one of nine planets that orbit the Sun. Moons are balls of rock or ice that orbit planets. Earth has just one moon. You can see it clearly on many nights, and sometimes during the day too. Some planets have many moons. For example, the planet Jupiter has at least 61.

Internet links

For a link to a website where you can take a 3-D tour, or click on the names of the planets for information, pictures, videos and games, go to **www.usborne-quicklinks.com**

Galaxy M81, shown here, is about 12 million light years from Earth. This photograph was taken by a giant telescope in Hawaii, USA.

Our Solar System

The Sun, the nine planets and their moons, and everything else that orbits the Sun, are together known as the Solar System. The Sun keeps everything in orbit around it with a pulling force called gravity. This is the same force that makes things fall to the ground when you drop them.

This diagram shows the paths the planets take as they orbit the Sun.

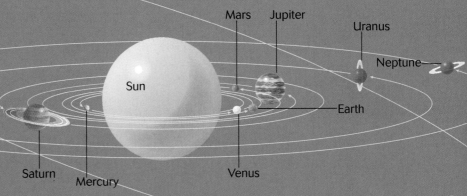

Pluto

Mars   Jupiter

Uranus

Neptune

Sun

Earth

Saturn

Mercury

Venus

Changing sky

What we can see in the sky is constantly changing. For example, the stars seem to change position during the course of a night, and we also see different stars at different times of the year. These changes are caused by the Earth's movements.

The camera used to take this photograph used a special technique to photograph the paths the stars take in the course of an evening. It shows the stars' movement as trails of light.

Spinning Earth

When you look out of the window of a fast-moving train, it looks as if things outside are moving in the opposite direction when, in fact, they are not moving at all. The spinning of the Earth creates the same effect. As it spins in one direction, the Sun and stars look as if they are moving in the opposite direction. But they are not really moving much at all.

The Earth spins around once every 24 hours. As it spins, it looks as if the stars, Sun and Moon are moving around it.

Fact: As the Earth orbits the Sun, it travels through 942,000,000km (588,750,000 miles) of space in a year.

Where on Earth?

It's not just the Earth's movement that affects which stars you can see, but also where you are on Earth. Scientists divide the Earth into two halves, known as the northern and the southern hemispheres. What you can see depends on which hemisphere you are in.

A group of stars known as the Plough (or the Big Dipper) is visible in the northern hemisphere, but not in the southern.

Northern hemisphere

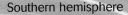

Southern hemisphere

The group of stars Crux is visible in the southern hemisphere, but not in the northern hemisphere.

Different views

We can see different stars at different times of the year. This is because, as the Earth travels through space as it orbits the Sun, different stars come into view. The Earth always orbits at roughly the same rate and in the same direction. So we can predict which stars we will be able to see at any particular time of the year.

Internet links

For a link to a website where you can find out more about how the Earth moves, go to **www.usborne-quicklinks.com**

Starting skywatching

You can see thousands of stars and some of the planets with just your own eyes. But if you use binoculars or a telescope, you'll be able to see much more, and things will look bigger, brighter and clearer.

Starting to look

If you are just beginning to learn about astronomy, binoculars are ideal for looking at the sky. They are not as powerful as telescopes, but they are cheaper and easier to use. They will enable you to see many different types of objects, including thousands of stars, and mountains and craters on the Moon.

Inside binoculars

Binoculars contain pieces of glass, called lenses. They have two types of lenses inside them: objective lenses and magnifying lenses. Objective lenses collect light from objects into the binoculars to form images. The light then travels down the binocular tubes to the magnifying lenses, which make the images look bigger. The objective lenses turn the images upside down, so binoculars also contain pieces of glass, called prisms, which turn them the right side up again.

These are the eyepieces that you look through to see images. They contain the magnifying lenses.

This diagram shows how light travels through binoculars.

Eyepiece

Magnifying lens

Prisms

The rays of light move in the direction of the arrows.

Objective lens

Ray of light

This is a pair of standard medium-weight binoculars.

There is an objective lens in this part of the binoculars.

Power and size

Binoculars come in different sizes and powers. For example, the binoculars shown above are 10x50. The first number tells you how much the binoculars can magnify images: these binoculars can make things look ten times bigger than they really are. The second number tells you the size of the objective lenses. Bigger objective lenses let more light into the binoculars and give brighter, clearer images.

Using binoculars

When using binoculars, always keep the strap around your neck so that you don't drop them. To get a clear image, it's important to hold them very still. You can help to steady your binoculars by sitting with your elbows on your knees, or resting your elbows on a wall. Alternatively, you can use a stand, such as a camera tripod.

You can steady your hands by resting your elbows on your knees.

You can also keep your binoculars still by leaning against a wall.

Internet links

For a link to a website where you can find some more tips on how to start skywatching, go to **www.usborne-quicklinks.com**

Watching the sky

The best time to observe the sky is on a dark, cloudless night. If possible, you should go to an open place where there are few street lights or, better still, none at all. Wear warm clothes, and take a pen and paper so that you can make a record of what you see. You should always go with a parent.

Fact: If you want to buy binoculars for star gazing, medium-sized standard binoculars ranging from 7x30 to 10x50 are good sizes to choose.

Using telescopes

Telescopes will enable you to see more detail than you can with binoculars, but they are more difficult to use. There are two main types of telescopes: refractor and reflector telescopes.

This diagram shows how light travels through a refractor telescope

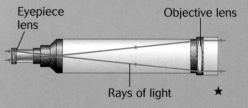

Eyepiece lens

Objective lens

Rays of light ★

Refractors and reflectors

Refractor telescopes work in a similar way to binoculars. They have an objective lens at one end, which collects light into the telescope tube, and a magnifying lens in the eyepiece at the other end.

Here you can see how light travels through a reflector telescope

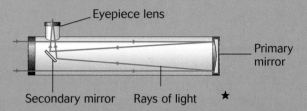

Eyepiece lens

Primary mirror

Secondary mirror   Rays of light ★

Reflector telescopes use mirrors to collect light. They have a primary mirror which collects light into the telescope, and a secondary mirror which directs the light into a magnifying lens in the eyepiece.

The telescope shown on these pages is a refractor telescope.

This is a finder, a small, low-power telescope that is attached to the main telescope. It's used to line up the main telescope with the object you want to look at.

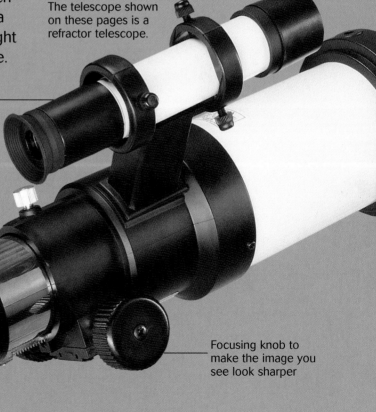

Eyepiece that you look through to see the image

Focusing knob to make the image you see look sharper

Different powers

The larger a telescope's objective lens or primary mirror is, the more powerful the telescope will be, and the more you will be able to see through it. If you want to buy a telescope, it's best to buy a refractor telescope with an objective lens that's at least 75mm (3 inches) across. Alternatively, you could buy a reflector with a primary mirror at least 115mm (4.5 inches) across.

The telescope's objective lens is inside here. This telescope has a 100mm (4 inch) objective lens.

Light enters the telescope here.

When the telescope is not in use, a protective cap is placed over this end of the telescope.

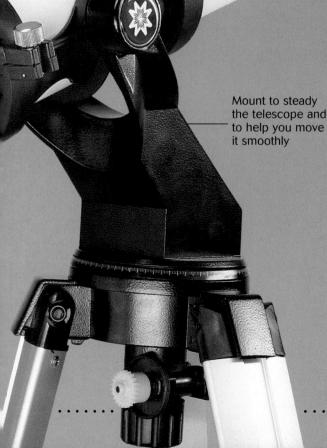

Mount to steady the telescope and to help you move it smoothly

Using your telescope

If you begin by using an eyepiece with a low magnification, you will be able to see a wide section of sky. This makes it easier to find things. Start by looking for a bright object, such as a star. To find it, line up your telescope with the small "finder" telescope on top of it. When the star is in the middle of the finder, it should be visible through the main eyepiece. If the star looks blurred, adjust the eyepiece by moving the focusing knob until you get a clear image.

Internet links

For a link to a website where you can find a guide to buying telescopes, go to **www.usborne-quicklinks.com**

Deeper into space ....

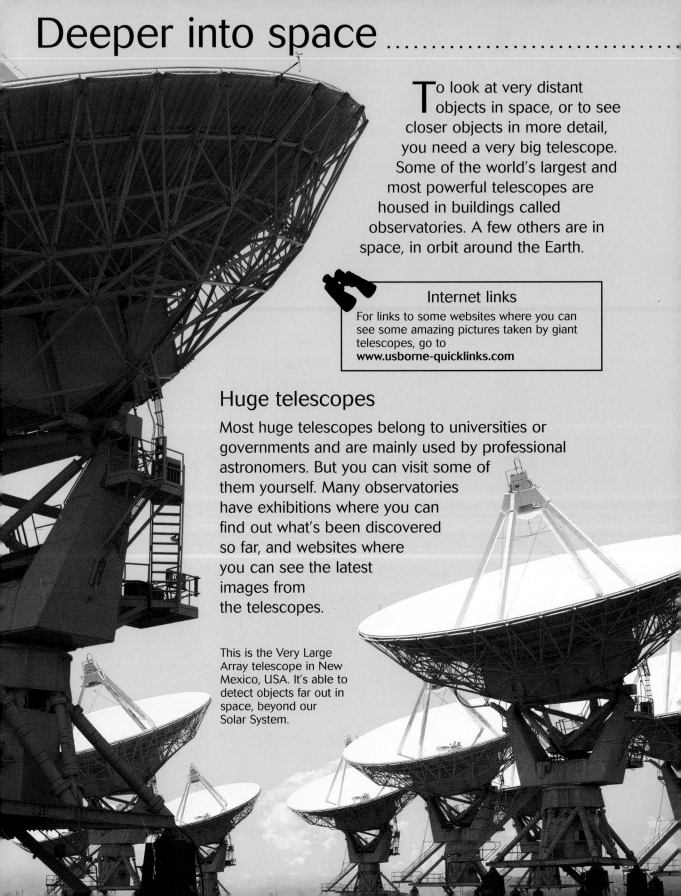

To look at very distant objects in space, or to see closer objects in more detail, you need a very big telescope. Some of the world's largest and most powerful telescopes are housed in buildings called observatories. A few others are in space, in orbit around the Earth.

Internet links

For links to some websites where you can see some amazing pictures taken by giant telescopes, go to
www.usborne-quicklinks.com

Huge telescopes

Most huge telescopes belong to universities or governments and are mainly used by professional astronomers. But you can visit some of them yourself. Many observatories have exhibitions where you can find out what's been discovered so far, and websites where you can see the latest images from the telescopes.

This is the Very Large Array telescope in New Mexico, USA. It's able to detect objects far out in space, beyond our Solar System.

Observatories

It's possible to see stars in very distant parts of the universe through these telescopes at the Keck Observatory in Hawaii, USA.

Observatories are often built high up on mountain tops, away from the glare of city lights. The Keck reflector telescopes, for example, are located 4km (2.5 miles) up a mountain in Hawaii. They are the largest telescopes in the world, with primary mirrors 8–10m (26–33ft) across.

Radio telescopes

Many objects in space, such as stars and galaxies, give out invisible signals called radio waves. Astronomers detect them using radio telescopes. By studying the signals, they can find out what these objects are made of and how they move.

These huge dishes collect signals from space. By linking many dishes together, astronomers can detect fainter signals than with just one dish.

Telescopes in space

In 1990, the Hubble Space Telescope was launched into space. It is a large reflector telescope with a 2.3m (7.5ft) primary mirror. It orbits the Earth every 90 minutes, at a height of about 595km (370 miles). Occasionally, you can see it moving across the night sky, looking like a faint star. You can see thousands of images from Hubble on the Internet.

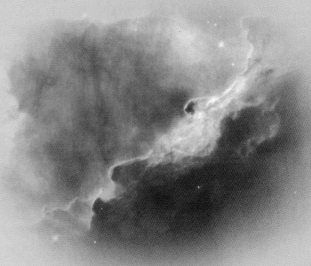

This photograph, taken by the Hubble Space Telescope, shows part of the Omega, or Swan, Nebula, about 5,500 light years away from Earth.

Space probes

Dozens of unmanned spacecraft, called probes, have been sent into space to explore our Solar System. Many carry cameras and have sent back amazing images of distant planets. Space probes *Voyager 1* and *Voyager 2* have gone farther than any other spacecraft. You can track their progress on the Internet.

The Sun

The Sun is a huge ball of burning gas which gives our planet light and heat. Without it, there would be no life on Earth. The Sun is about 1.4 million km (870,000 miles) across — you could fit one million planets the size of Earth inside it.

This image of the Sun was made at the SOHO observatory in space.

Observing the Sun

There are many interesting features on the Sun's surface that you can see from Earth. But the Sun is so bright that if you looked at it you would permanently damage your eyes, and could even go blind. There are some safe ways of looking at the Sun. The easiest method is to project the Sun's image onto some cardboard.

You can project an image of the Sun with binoculars. Put the cap on one side of the binoculars and point the eyepieces at a piece of cardboard.

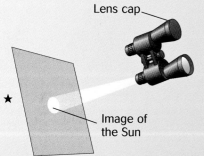

Lens cap

Sun

★

Image of the Sun

Do not look directly at the Sun or through the binoculars at any point.

If you point the other end of the binoculars at the Sun, you should see the Sun projected onto the cardboard as a bright circle of light. You can then focus the binoculars to get a sharper image.

Using filters

You can also look at the Sun through a telescope, using filters that have been designed to protect your eyes from the Sun. But you should only buy filters from a specialist telescope shop and should ask for advice before you buy. Only use filters that fit over the front of the telescope. Cheaper filters that screw into the eyepiece may crack, allowing sunlight into your eyes.

Fact: Temperatures inside the Sun reach over 15 million°C (27 million°F). That's about 60,000 times hotter than the highest temperature of an oven.

Loops and flares

Enormous loops of glowing gas, called prominences, leap from the Sun at high speeds. They usually last for just a few hours and are quite difficult to see. But you can see them during solar eclipses (see pages 18–19) using a safe method of looking at the Sun. Occasionally, incredibly hot jets of burning gases also explode out of the Sun. These are known as solar flares.

Solar prominences like this one can extend for up to 30,000km (50,000 miles) from the Sun.

Internet links

For a link to a website where you can take a virtual tour of the Sun, go to **www.usborne-quicklinks.com**

Sunspots

Using a safe way of looking at the Sun, you may be able to see dark spots on its surface, known as sunspots. These are areas that are cooler than the rest of the Sun. Sunspots have an average temperature of 4,000°C (7,000°F). The average temperature elsewhere on the surface of the Sun is 5,500°C (9,900°F).

This is a close-up view of sunspots. They often form in groups like this.

The Moon

The Moon is the second-brightest object in the sky. It's close enough to Earth for you to be able to see many of its features with binoculars or a small telescope.

This photograph was taken by space probe *Galileo*. It clearly shows some of the Moon's features, including craters, *montes* (mountains) and *maria*.

Crater Plato

Montes Jura

Craters

The Moon is covered with millions of hollows, or craters, which were made by large objects crashing into its surface. Most are less than 15km (10 miles) across. But a few are so big that you can see them with the naked eye on a clear night.

This is a picture of Copernicus, one of the Moon's largest craters. It is 90km (56 miles) across. The specks you can see inside it are mountains.

Oceanus Procellarum

Crater Archimedes

Crater Copernicus

Mountains and maria

When you look at the Moon, you will see light and dark patches. The dark patches are known as *maria* (singular: *mare*). Early astronomers thought that they were seas – *maria* means "seas" in Latin. In fact, they are areas which were once flooded with molten rock, called lava, that seeped out from inside the Moon, and then cooled and hardened. The light patches are mountains, or *montes*.

Crater Tycho

Fact: The Moon formed many billions of years ago when a very large object crashed into the Earth. The debris from the impact became the Moon.

One-sided view

The Moon spins around as it orbits the Earth. It takes exactly the same amount of time to spin around once as the Earth does. Because of this, we can only ever see one side of the Moon from Earth. The side of the Moon that faces away from us is known as the "dark side of the Moon".

This photograph of a crater on the far side of the Moon was taken by US astronauts on spacecraft *Apollo 11*.

Mare Serenitatis

People landed on the Moon for the first time in *Mare Tranquillitatis.*

Mare Crisium

Mare Nectaris

Mare Fecunditatis

These lines, streaking away from crater Tycho, are made from rocks and dust. The rocks and dust were flung outwards when the large object that made Tycho hit the Moon.

Changing shape

Although the Moon looks bright, it doesn't give out any light of its own. The light we see is sunlight reflecting off its surface. As the Moon orbits the Earth, we see different amounts of its sunlit side, which makes the Moon seem to change shape. These changes are known as the phases of the Moon.

Here you can see what the Moon looks like during eight of its phases.

New Moon   Waxing Crescent   First Quarter   Waxing Gibbous

Full Moon   Waning Gibbous   Last Quarter   Waning Crescent

Eclipses ....

As the Earth and Moon move, they sometimes block off sunlight from each other. This is called an eclipse. Eclipses are dramatic events that are easy to observe, although they don't happen very often. There are two types of eclipses – solar (of the Sun) and lunar (of the Moon).

Solar eclipses

Solar eclipses happen when the Moon lies between Earth and the Sun and makes a shadow on part of the Earth's surface. Even though the Moon is much smaller than the Sun, it is also much nearer. This means that it looks as big as the Sun. So, when it's between Earth and the Sun, it is able to block out the Sun's light.

This is a total eclipse of the Sun. The blue light you can see around the Moon is the Sun's atmosphere, or corona. It's made of gases and it surrounds the Sun.

In the Moon's shadow

You can only see a solar eclipse if you are in a part of the world that's in the Moon's shadow. In the outer part of the shadow, called the penumbra, only some of the Sun's light is blocked out. This is a partial solar eclipse. When this happens, the Sun looks as if a bite has been taken out of it. In the inner part of the shadow, called the umbra, the Moon completely covers the Sun and all light is blocked out. This is a total solar eclipse.

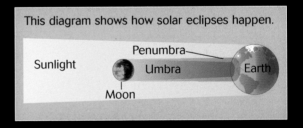

This diagram shows how solar eclipses happen.

Sunlight · Penumbra · Umbra · Earth · Moon

Internet links

For a link to a website where you can see images and watch movies of eclipses, and find out about future eclipses, go to **www.usborne-quicklinks.com**

Fact: In some countries people believe solar eclipses are caused by a dragon eating the Sun, so they make lots of noise to scare it away and bring the Sun back.

Annular eclipses

During some solar eclipses, the Moon doesn't cover the Sun completely and you can still see a ring of sunlight around the Moon. These eclipses are known as annular eclipses. They happen when the Moon is at its farthest point away from the Earth, when it looks slightly smaller than the Sun.

During annular eclipses, like the one shown here, it's not possible to see the Sun's corona. But you can see a ring of sunlight around the Moon.

Lunar eclipses

Lunar eclipses happen when the Earth is between the Sun and the Moon, and the Moon moves into the Earth's shadow. When the Moon passes through the Earth's umbra, there's a total lunar eclipse. When only part of it passes through the umbra, there's a partial lunar eclipse.

Warning

When viewing a solar eclipse, only ever use a safe method of looking at the Sun (see page 14). Even looking at just a little direct sunlight will damage your eyes.

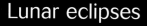

Viewing lunar eclipses

The Moon is still visible during a lunar eclipse even if it's a total one. It looks very dark and has a reddish glow. Lunar eclipses look the same wherever you are on Earth and it's safe to watch them without taking any special precautions.

The Moon here is completely covered during a total lunar eclipse, making it look orange.

Stars ....

Stars start their lives in swirling clouds of gas and dust, called *nebulae*. They can live for billions of years and, during their lifespan, change in size, brightness and shade until they eventually die.

Red, white and blue

Stars are divided into different categories according to how hot their surfaces are. The hottest stars usually look white or blue, and the coolest ones generally look red. The different categories are called spectral types and they are identified by letters.

Here you can see the main spectral types. O-type stars are the hottest, and M-type stars the coolest.

Star brightness

Some stars shine more brightly than others. Their brightness is measured on a scale called magnitude. Some stars shine very brightly, but they just look dim, as they are very far away. Because of this, astronomers distinguish between apparent magnitude (how bright they *look*) and absolute magnitude (how bright stars really *are*). The brightest stars have a magnitude of 0 or less.

Double stars

Some stars appear to have one or more companion stars. Stars with one companion are known as double stars. Some double stars aren't really anywhere near each other – they just look as if they are from Earth. But others are relatively close to one another and some are even in orbit around each other. You can see many double stars using a small telescope.

The two stars at the top here make up double star system *Zeta Scorpii*. The stars seem to line up, but are not, in fact, close to each other.

Internet links

For a link to a website where you can find out about different types of stars, go to **www.usborne-quicklinks.com**

Fact: The nearest star to our Solar System is *Proxima Centauri*. It's 4.2 light years away.

This is star cluster *Omega Centauri*, located about 16,000 light years away. It is one of the brightest globular clusters in our galaxy and contains over a million stars.

Star clusters

Stars are often grouped together in clusters. There are two types of clusters: open and globular. Open clusters are made up of very bright, young stars, quite widely spaced apart. There can be anything from ten to 1,000 stars in an open cluster. Some of the larger ones, such as the Pleiades, are bright enough to see with the naked eye. Globular clusters contain massive numbers of old stars tightly packed together. With a small telescope they look like fuzzy balls of light. Most of the ones we can see are on the outskirts of our galaxy.

Galaxies ....

Stars are grouped together in galaxies. There are billions of galaxies in the universe, each containing billions of stars. Our Solar System is a tiny part of a galaxy called the Milky Way.

This is galaxy NGC 1232. It's 100 million light years away from our galaxy.

Internet links

For a link to a website where you can become a galaxy hunter and go on a photographic tour of the galaxies, go to **www.usborne-quicklinks.com**

Galaxy shapes

Galaxies have different shapes. Spiral, barred spiral and elliptical are the most common shapes. Some galaxies have no fixed shape and are known as irregular galaxies. Even through a small telescope, there are lots of galaxies you can see. They look like blurred smudges of light. But, with a more powerful telescope, you will be able to see the shapes of some of them.

Spiral galaxies have a bright middle with two or more curved arms of stars spiralling out from it.

Barred spiral galaxies have a bar across the bright middle with an arm at each end of the bar.

Elliptical galaxies can be round, oval, like the one shown here, or even sausage-shaped.

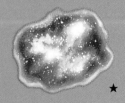

Irregular galaxies, such as this one, are often formed when one galaxy crashes into another.

Our galaxy

Because our planet lies within the Milky Way, we can't see it from the outside and it's difficult to tell exactly what shape it is. But most astronomers think that it's spiral-shaped. Compared to many other galaxies, it's large. It is about 100,000 light years across and it contains two thousand billion* stars.

* US = trillion

Observing the Milky Way

You can see part of the Milky Way with the naked eye. It looks like a broad, dense band of stars. On clear nights, you can see dark trails of dust and brighter star clouds within the band. The best time to look is July to September in the northern hemisphere, and October to December in the southern hemisphere.

This photograph of the Milky Way was taken in Arizona, USA.

Groups of galaxies

Like stars, galaxies are grouped together in clusters. Our galaxy is in a cluster called the Local Group. It contains two other large galaxies and about 30 smaller galaxies, and is five million light years across. It's quite a small cluster compared to others. Amazingly, some contain as many as 2,500 galaxies.

This is a photograph of galaxy cluster Abell 1689, taken by the Hubble Space Telescope. It's one of the biggest clusters of galaxies that has been discovered so far.

Star patterns

For thousands of years, people have seen patterns in the stars. These are known as constellations. They are made up of the brightest stars in the sky and the area of sky around them.

Ancient names

There are 88 official constellations. Many have animal names, or the names of characters from ancient Greek mythology. If you draw imaginary lines between the main stars in a constellation, you may be able to see the shape of the animal, person or object they were named after.

Cygnus is the Latin for "swan". Early astronomers thought that the constellation looked like a bird.

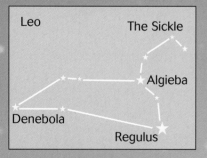

Leo is Latin for "lion". The part of it known as the Sickle represents the lion's head.

Near and far

The stars in constellations look as if they are close together, but in fact they are very far apart from each other. They are also at vastly different distances from the Earth.

This is how the stars in Orion appear to us from Earth. They all seem to be the same distance away.

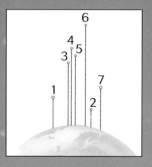

This diagram shows the actual relative distances between the stars in Orion and Earth

Constellation Crux is the smallest constellation in the sky.

Smaller groups

Smaller patterns, called asterisms, are made from part of a constellation, or from stars from different constellations. For example, the Plough (also known as the Big Dipper) is an asterism which is part of the constellation Ursa Major.

This is the Plough asterism. It looks as if it's made up of seven stars. But in fact, one of the seven stars is a double star.

Orion contains many bright stars, including Rigel, which is the seventh-brightest star in the night sky. It also contains the asterism Orion's Belt.

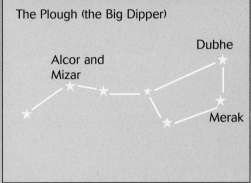

The Plough (the Big Dipper)

Dubhe

Alcor and Mizar

Merak

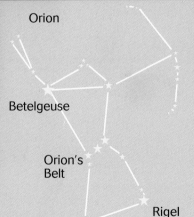

Orion

Betelgeuse

Orion's Belt

Rigel

Star charts

It isn't always easy to find constellations. But you can use star charts to help you. These tell you where constellations and stars are at different times of the year and in different hemispheres. On the next eight pages, you will find some star charts. To use them, choose the correct hemisphere and time of year, and look in the direction indicated at the bottom of the chart.

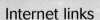

Internet links

For a link to a website where you can find a detailed guide to the constellations, go to www.usborne-quicklinks.com

March to May

Maps for the northern hemisphere

Best times to look:
March 15th at 11pm
April 15th at 9pm
May 15th at 10pm

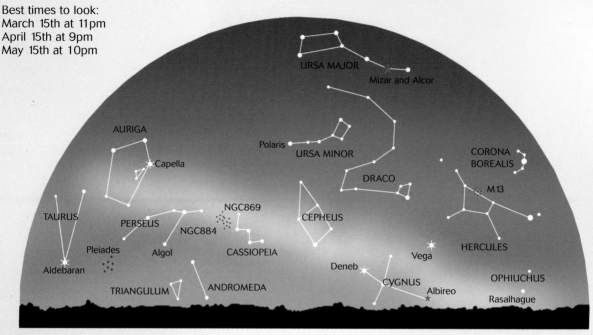

West   Looking north   East

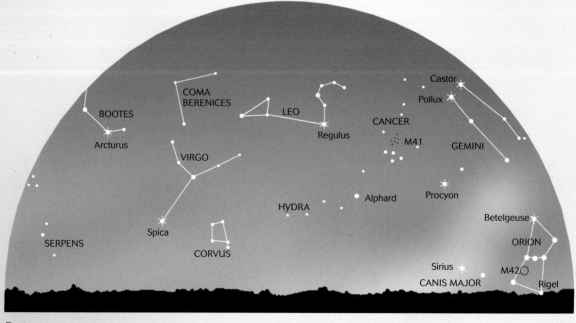

East   Looking south   West

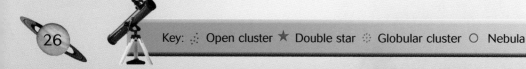

Key: ⠿ Open cluster ★ Double star ⁙ Globular cluster ○ Nebula ⌣ Galaxy

Maps for the southern hemisphere

Best times to look:
March 15th at 11pm
April 15th at 10pm
May 15th at 8pm

West   Looking north   East

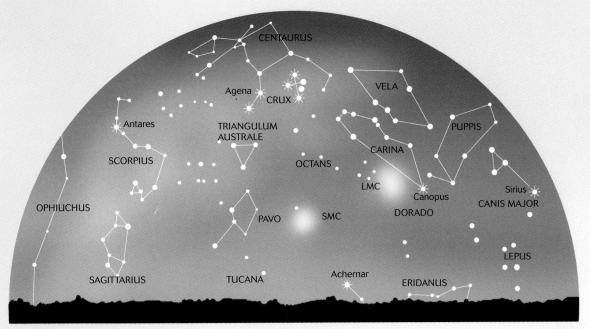

East   Looking south   West

March to May meteor showers: Lyrids, April 18th to 22nd. Spring Aquarids, May 2nd to 7th.

27

June to August

Maps for the northern hemisphere

Best times to look:
June 15th at 2am
July 15th at midnight
August 15th at 10pm

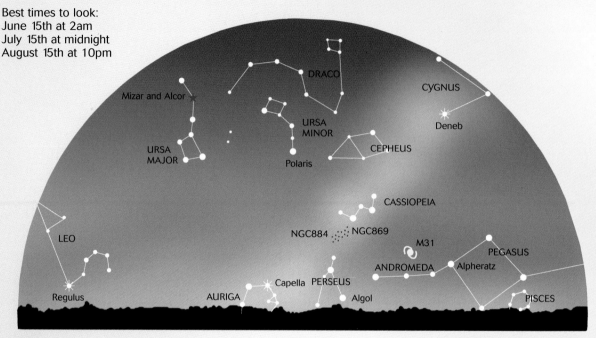

West — Looking north — East

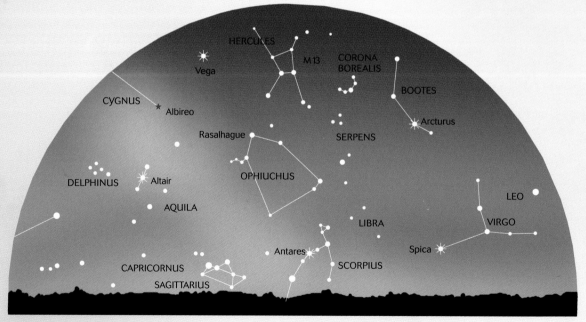

East — Looking south — West

Key: ∴ Open cluster ★ Double star ⁛ Globular cluster ○ Nebula ⌇ Galaxy

Maps for the southern hemisphere

Best times to look:
June 15th at midnight
July 15th at 10pm
August 15th at 8pm

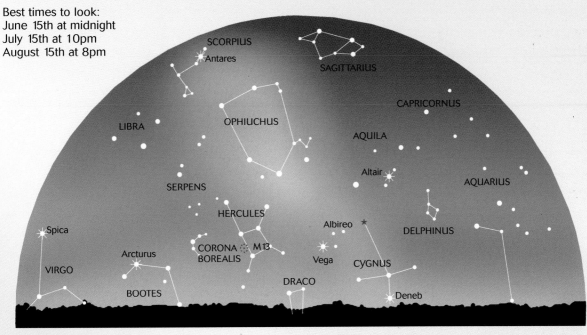

SCORPIUS
Antares
SAGITTARIUS
CAPRICORNUS
LIBRA
OPHIUCHUS
AQUILA
Altair
AQUARIUS
SERPENS
HERCULES
Albireo
DELPHINUS
Spica
CORONA · M13
BOREALIS
Vega
CYGNUS
Arcturus
VIRGO
DRACO
Deneb
BOOTES

West | Looking north | East

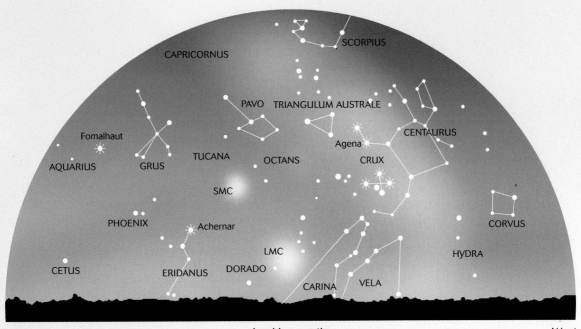

SCORPIUS
CAPRICORNUS
PAVO TRIANGULUM AUSTRALE
Fomalhaut
CENTAURUS
Agena
TUCANA OCTANS CRUX
AQUARIUS
GRUS
SMC
CORVUS
PHOENIX Achernar
HYDRA
LMC
CETUS ERIDANUS DORADO
CARINA VELA

East | Looking south | West

June to August meteor showers: Summer Aquarids, July 26th to 31st.
Perseids, August 10th to 14th.

29

September to November ....

Maps for the northern hemisphere

Best times to look:
September 15th at 11pm
October 15th at 10pm
November 15th at 8pm

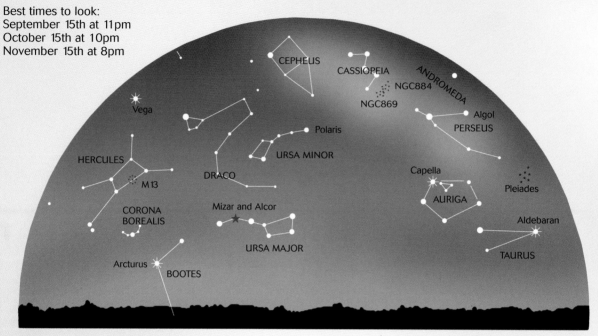

CEPHEUS

CASSIOPEIA

ANDROMEDA

NGC884

NGC869

Vega

Algol

PERSEUS

Polaris

URSA MINOR

HERCULES

Capella

Pleiades

M13

DRACO

AURIGA

CORONA
BOREALIS

Mizar and Alcor

Aldebaran

URSA MAJOR

TAURUS

Arcturus

BOOTES

West   Looking north   East

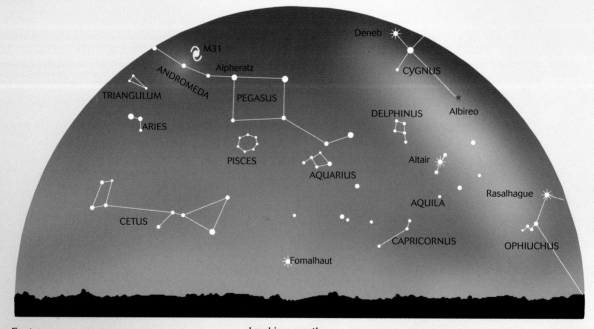

Deneb

M31

Alpheratz

ANDROMEDA

CYGNUS

PEGASUS

TRIANGULUM

DELPHINUS

Albireo

ARIES

PISCES

Altair

AQUARIUS

AQUILA

Rasalhague

CETUS

CAPRICORNUS

OPHIUCHUS

Fomalhaut

East   Looking south   West

30

Key: ∵ Open cluster ★ Double star ∷ Globular cluster ○ Nebula ℮ Galaxy

Maps for the southern hemisphere

Best times to look:
September 15th at midnight
October 15th at 10pm
November 15th at 8pm

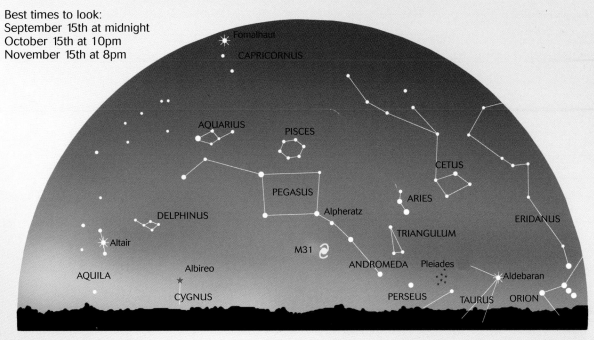

Formalhaut
CAPRICORNUS
AQUARIUS
PISCES
CETUS
ARIES
PEGASUS
Alpheratz
ERIDANUS
DELPHINUS
TRIANGULUM
Altair
M31
ANDROMEDA
Pleiades
AQUILA
Albireo
Aldebaran
CYGNUS
PERSEUS
TAURUS
ORION

West   Looking north   East

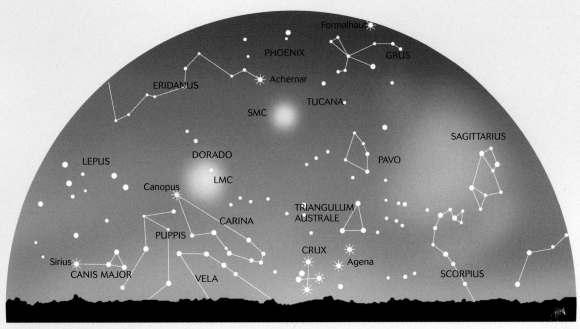

Formalhaut
PHOENIX
GRUS
ERIDANUS
Achernar
TUCANA
SMC
SAGITTARIUS
LEPUS
DORADO
PAVO
LMC
Canopus
TRIANGULUM
AUSTRALE
CARINA
PUPPIS
CRUX
Sirius
Agena
CANIS MAJOR
VELA
SCORPIUS

East   Looking south   West

September to November meteor showers: Orionids, October 18th to 23rd.
Taurids, November 1st to 7th. Leonids, November 14th to 19th.

December to February ....

Maps for the northern hemisphere

Best times to look:
December 15th at 11pm
January 15th at 9pm
February 15th at 7pm

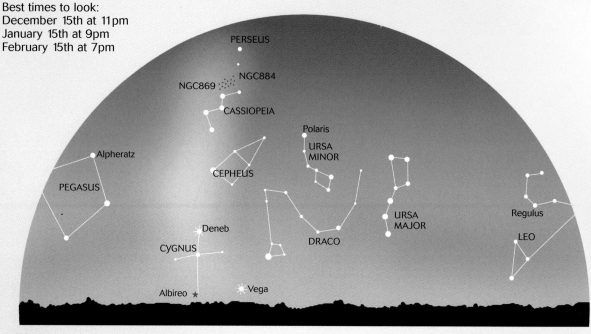

PERSEUS

NGC884

NGC869

CASSIOPEIA

Polaris

URSA MINOR

Alpheratz

CEPHEUS

PEGASUS

Regulus

URSA MAJOR

LEO

Deneb

CYGNUS

DRACO

Albireo ★   Vega

West   **Looking north**   East

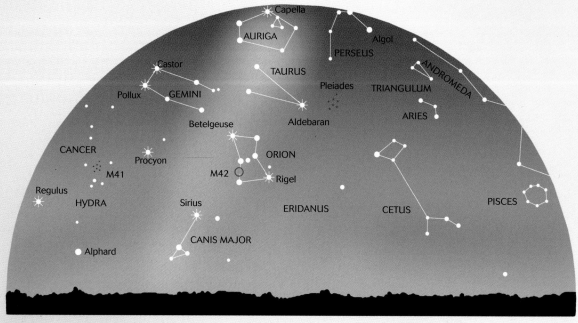

Capella

AURIGA

Algol

PERSEUS

TAURUS

ANDROMEDA

Castor

Pleiades

TRIANGULUM

Pollux   GEMINI

Aldebaran

ARIES

Betelgeuse

CANCER

Procyon

ORION

M41

M42   Rigel

Regulus

HYDRA

Sirius

ERIDANUS

CETUS

PISCES

Alphard

CANIS MAJOR

East   **Looking south**   West

32

Key: ⁖ Open cluster ★ Double star ⁖ Globular cluster ○ Nebula ⬭ Galaxy

Maps for the southern hemisphere

Best times to look:
December 15th at 11pm
January 15th at 9pm
February 15th at 8pm

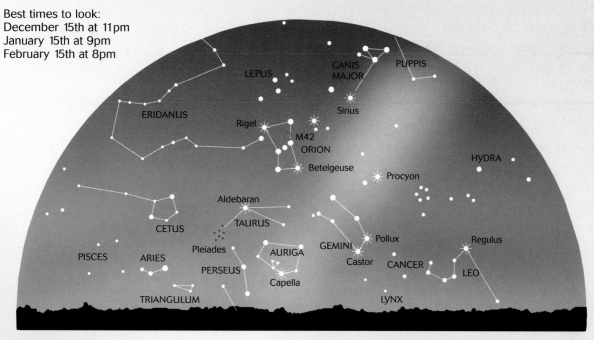

PUPPIS

CANIS MAJOR

LEPUS

Sirius

ERIDANUS

Rigel

M42

ORION

Betelgeuse

HYDRA

Procyon

Aldebaran

TAURUS

CETUS

Pleiades

GEMINI

Pollux

Regulus

PISCES

ARIES

PERSEUS

AURIGA

Castor

CANCER

LEO

Capella

LYNX

TRIANGULUM

West   Looking north   East

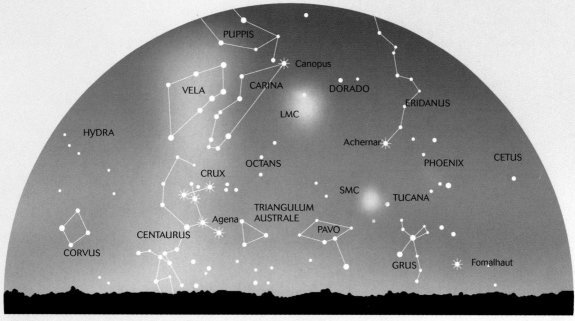

PUPPIS

Canopus

VELA

CARINA

DORADO

ERIDANUS

LMC

HYDRA

Achernar

CETUS

OCTANS

PHOENIX

CRUX

SMC

TUCANA

TRIANGULUM AUSTRALE

Agena

PAVO

CENTAURUS

GRUS

Fomalhaut

CORVUS

East   Looking south   West

December to February meteor showers: Geminids, December 10th to 13th.
Quadrantids, January 2nd to 4th.

33

Planet watching

Five of the planets in our Solar System can be seen easily from Earth without using any special equipment. They look very similar to stars in the night sky but, unlike stars, planets do not twinkle.

This diagram shows the Sun and nine planets of our Solar System. (They are not shown to scale here.)

Jupiter

Venus

Mars

Mercury

Sun

Earth

Uranus

Pluto

Finding the planets

Like Earth, all the planets in the Solar System orbit the Sun. Each planet takes a different amount of time to do this. This means that they are not in the same place at the same time every year. So you need a different planet chart each month to find them. You can find out the current positions of the planets on the Internet, and in newspapers or monthly astronomy magazines.

Internet links

For a link to a website where you can find out where the planets are at any time and from any location on Earth, go to **www.usborne-quicklinks.com**

Inner planets

Astronomers divide the planets into two groups: the inner and the outer planets. The inner planets are the four closest to the Sun: Mercury, Venus, Earth and Mars. They are all small and rocky.

Outer planets

The outer planets are Jupiter, Saturn, Uranus, Neptune and Pluto. Jupiter, Saturn, Uranus and Neptune are made up of ice, gas and liquids and are known as gas giants. Pluto is much smaller and is made of rock, ice and frozen gas.

Saturn

Neptune

Observing the planets

Mercury and Venus are closer to the Sun than Earth is. For a lot of the time, if we tried to look at them, we would be looking at the Sun, and they would be difficult to see in the Sun's glare. So the best time to observe them is when they are far to the east or west of the Sun. When this happens, they are "at elongation". The other six planets are best seen when they are directly opposite the Sun, with the Earth between them and the Sun. When they are in this position they are "at opposition".

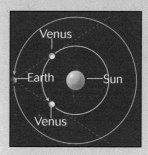

This diagram shows the positions of Venus when it's at elongation.

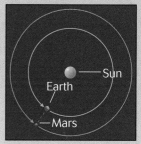

Here you can see the position of Mars when it's at opposition.

Moving backwards

Although all the planets always move in the same direction, Mars, Jupiter, Saturn, Uranus, Neptune and Pluto sometimes seem to change direction. This is known as retrograde motion. It happens because Earth orbits the Sun faster than these planets do and sometimes overtakes one of them. When it does this, the other planet looks as if it is moving backwards through the sky.

Mercury and Venus ....

Venus is the brightest of all the planets and is easy to see even without binoculars or a telescope. When it's visible, you can see it in the early morning or in the early evening. Mercury is far more difficult to see. Because it's very close to the Sun, it's usually hidden in the Sun's glare.

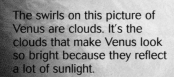

The swirls on this picture of Venus are clouds. It's the clouds that make Venus look so bright because they reflect a lot of sunlight.

Hidden surface

Even though Venus is easy to see, it's impossible to see any of its surface features from Earth because it's covered with a thick layer of clouds. Photographs of its surface taken by space probes show that it has a rocky surface, with mountains, canyons, shallow craters, volcanoes and hardened lava flows.

Looking for Mercury

Several times a year, Mercury is far enough away from the Sun for you to see it. It can be seen either just before sunrise or just after sunset, very low in the sky. But you can't see any details of Mercury's surface from Earth even with a very powerful telescope.

In transit

When the Sun, Mercury and Earth are lined up with each other, Mercury appears to move across the Sun. This is known as a transit of Mercury. Using a safe method of looking at the Sun, you can see Mercury as a tiny black dot on the Sun's surface.

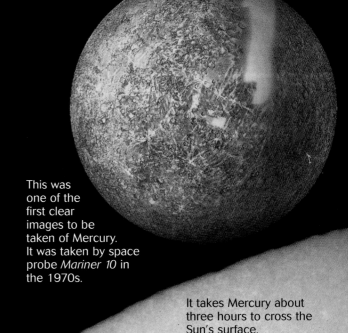

This was one of the first clear images to be taken of Mercury. It was taken by space probe *Mariner 10* in the 1970s.

It takes Mercury about three hours to cross the Sun's surface.

Mars ....

Mars is the closest planet to Earth. It appears as a small, pinkish-red light in the night sky. It looks red because of the red iron-rich dust and rock that cover most of its surface. The best time to see Mars is when it's close to Earth and opposite the Sun. This happens about once every two years.

This photograph of Mars was taken by the Hubble Space Telescope in August 2003. At this time, Mars was closer to Earth than it had been in the last 60,000 years.

Ice cap

Surface features

Mars's surface is covered with craters and canyons. Canyon *Valles Marineris* is the largest canyon in the Solar System. If it were on Earth, it would stretch all the way from London to New York. Mars also has several extinct volcanoes. *Olympus Mons* is the biggest. It's an amazing 24km (15 miles) high and 550km (342 miles) across.

This is a close-up view of *Olympus Mons*. It's three times higher than Mount Everest, Earth's highest mountain.

Ice caps

Like Earth, Mars has permanent ice caps at its poles. When you look at them through a telescope, you can see them as two large white patches. They are made of frozen carbon dioxide (also known as dry ice) and frozen water.

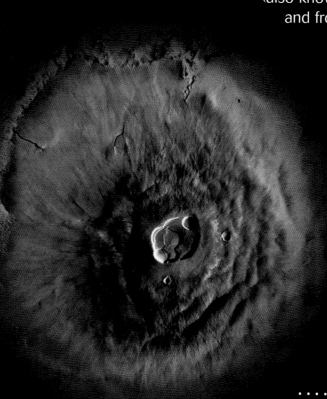

Jupiter and Saturn

Jupiter and Saturn are the largest planets in the Solar System and can be easily seen with the naked eye. They are both gas giants and have rings around them, although only Saturn's are easily visible from Earth.

Observing Jupiter

Jupiter is the fourth-brightest light in the night sky and is one of the easiest planets to see. It's a cloudy planet with lots of storms raging in its atmosphere. You can see light and dark bands of clouds, known as zones and belts, with just a small telescope. Dark and light patches within the bands are storms.

This photograph of Jupiter was taken by space probe *Voyager 1*.

Belt

Storms

Zone

Great Red Spot

Storms

The Great Red Spot

A huge storm has been visible on Jupiter for more than 300 years. It looks like a large, red oval and is known as the Great Red Spot. It changes slightly in size and shape from one year to the next and, at its largest, it's about three times the size of Earth.

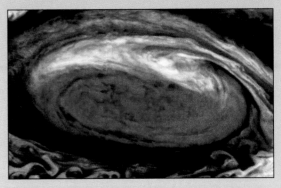

This close-up photograph of the Great Red Spot has been artificially tinted so that you can see the storm more clearly.

Jupiter's moons

So far, astronomers have discovered 61 moons in orbit around Jupiter. They vary in size from about 8km (6 miles) to 2,630km (1,750 miles) across. You can see the four largest moons – Ganymede, Callisto, Io and Europa – through binoculars.

Ganymede is the largest moon in the Solar System. It has many craters and it's covered with ice.

Golden Saturn

Saturn looks like a bright, golden star in the night sky. It is famous for its rings, which are made up of millions of pieces of ice and ice-covered rocks. The rings stretch out from Saturn for about 480,000km (300,000 miles). Saturn takes 29 years to orbit the Sun and as it does so our view of its rings changes.

When Earth faces the edges of Saturn's rings, you can hardly see them at all. They look like a dark line across the planet.

You can see this view of Saturn's rings, from above, when Saturn's north pole is tilted towards the Sun.

This view of Saturn's rings, from below, is visible when Saturn's south pole is tilted towards the Sun.

Fierce storms

Like Jupiter, Saturn has frequent, violent storms. They can be seen through a powerful telescope as swirls and spots in Saturn's yellow and gold cloud bands. Winds can reach speeds of up to 1,800kph (1,120mph). Even the strongest and most destructive winds on Earth only reach speeds of 250kph (155mph).

Saturn's moons

Saturn has at least 31 moons, although we can only see ten of them from Earth. Some of the smaller moons orbit Saturn inside its outermost rings. They are known as Shepherd Moons. Their gravity helps to keep the rings in place. The larger moons are visible as tiny dots of light orbiting the planet.

Fact: Scientists think that it's possible that there is very primitive life on Saturn's largest moon, Titan.

The outer planets

U ranus, Neptune and Pluto are the farthest planets from the Sun and are the most difficult to observe from Earth. Uranus can just about be seen with the naked eye. Neptune can only be seen with binoculars or a telescope and Pluto can only be seen through a very powerful telescope.

Uranus

Uranus is a gas planet. Its atmosphere contains large quantities of methane gas, which makes the planet look greeny-blue. Unlike other planets in our Solar System, Uranus orbits the Sun on its side. Astronomers think that Uranus was knocked into this position when a large object collided with it long ago.

Uranus's moons

So far, astronomers have discovered 27 moons orbiting Uranus. The largest is Titania, which is about half the size of Earth's moon. Some of the moons were discovered from Earth with powerful telescopes. Others were found by spacecraft *Voyager 2*.

Uranus has rings, as do all the other gas planets in our Solar System, but they are not easy to see from Earth.

Like all of Uranus's moons, Miranda is about 50% ice and 50% rock.

Oberon's surface is covered with craters.

Here you can see Uranus's five largest moons. (They are not shown to scale.)

Umbriel, like Oberon, is heavily cratered.

Ariel has many deep valleys as well as craters.

Titania is similar to Ariel, but is 35% bigger.

Internet links

For a link to a website where you can follow the progress of *Voyager 2*'s mission to Uranus and Neptune, go to **www.usborne-quicklinks.com**

Tiny Pluto

Astronomers don't know as much about Pluto as they do about the other planets. It is the farthest planet from the Sun for most of the time and it's also the smallest planet in the Solar System. It's too small and too far away for us to be able to see its surface features clearly from Earth. It is also the only planet that we haven't sent a space probe to.

Neptune

Through a telescope, Neptune looks like a tiny blue star. We learned most of what we know about it from images sent back to Earth by *Voyager 2*. It is another gas planet, with a system of rings which are too faint to see from Earth. Neptune has 11 moons. The biggest, Triton, is larger than Pluto. Unlike most moons, Triton orbits in the opposite direction to Neptune's spin.

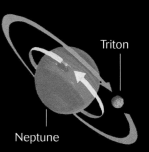

Triton

Neptune

This diagram shows the direction of Triton's orbit compared to the direction of Neptune's spin.

Great Dark Spot

Stormy Neptune

In 1989, *Voyager 2* sent images back of a storm raging in Neptune's atmosphere. It was about half the size of Jupiter's Great Red Spot and was named the Great Dark Spot. But in 1994, it suddenly disappeared from view. Astronomers are not sure whether the storm broke up, or if it just comes and goes from time to time.

This is a photograph of Neptune, taken by *Voyager 2* when the Great Dark Spot was still clearly visible.

Fact: Pluto is so small that some astronomers think that it isn't a planet at all.

41

Small bodies

As well as stars and planets, there are many smaller objects in space to look for, including comets, meteoroids and asteroids. When they come close enough to Earth, you can even see some of them with the naked eye.

Shooting stars

You might see bright streaks of light in the night sky that last for just a few seconds. These are meteors, or shooting stars. They're small pieces of rock and dust in space, called meteoroids, which burn up as they enter the Earth's atmosphere. As they burn, you can see them as fast-moving, bright streaks.

Meteor showers

Several times a year, you may be able to see exciting displays of lots of shooting stars. This is known as a meteor shower. Meteor showers happen when the Earth passes through trails of meteoroids. During a meteor shower you can see several shooting stars a minute.

This is a photograph of the Leonids meteor shower. You can see the shower in mid-November every year in both hemispheres.

Internet links

For a link to a website where you can find out more about comet tails and try making a comet, go to **www.usborne-quicklinks.com**

Icy comets

Comets are huge lumps of dirty ice, dust and grit that orbit the Sun. As they get closer to the Sun, the ice begins to melt and clouds of dust and gases, called comas, form around them. Some of the gas and dust streams out behind the comet to form "tails".

This is comet Hale-Bopp. It was clearly visible in 1997, when it came as close as 122 million miles to Earth. It probably won't return to Earth for another 2,300 years.

Comet watching

Every year, a few comets come close enough to Earth for us to see them through a telescope. They usually look like fuzzy stars, but occasionally a comet comes close enough for its tail to be visible. The most recent comet to come that close to Earth was Hale-Bopp. It was easy to see without a telescope for several months in 1997.

Asteroids

Asteroids are large pieces of rock and metal. Most of them orbit the Sun between Mars and Jupiter, in an area known as the Asteroid Belt. But some are much closer to Earth, and there are at least 200 that cross Earth's orbit. You can see dozens of them with a telescope. They look like points of light in the night sky.

Fact: Occasionally, very big meteoroids pass through the atmosphere and fall to Earth without burning up. These meteoroids are known as meteorites.

Sky sights ....

There are a lot of other exciting things to see in the night sky. For example, with a telescope you can observe the birthplaces of stars, far out in space. Much closer to Earth, you can spot man-made objects orbiting our planet, or gaze at mysterious lights near the north and south poles.

This *aurora* is happening near the north pole and is known as the *aurora borealis*, or northern lights. In the southern hemisphere, *aurorae* are known as the *aurora australis*, or southern lights.

Nebulae

Nebulae are swirling clouds of dust and gas, sometimes known as star nurseries, because new stars form there. You need a telescope to see most of them. Some look like dark patches of starless sky, while others are bright and surrounded by bright clouds of glowing gases.

This is the Orion Nebula. It looks bright because it's lit up by young bright stars within it.

Light show

Blue, red, green and white lights often light up the sky near the north and south poles. These are known as *aurorae* (singular: *aurora*). They are caused by the solar wind. This is a stream of invisible particles which the Sun is constantly blowing out into space. When the particles reach the Earth's atmosphere, they react with the gases in it, sometimes resulting in spectacular *aurorae*.

Satellites

There are many man-made objects, or artificial satellites, in orbit around Earth. Some are used to send television and radio signals from one part of the world to another. Others have telescopes on them for studying space. Many are covered with shiny metal that reflects sunlight. This means that you can sometimes see them from Earth and track their movements. Watch for points of white light moving across the sky.

Space explosions

Stars need a steady supply of gas to keep burning. Eventually they run out of gas and die. When some very big stars come to the end of their lives, they swell up and then explode spectacularly. This is called a *supernova*. Only four *supernovae* have been visible with the naked eye in the last 1,000 years. The most recent was in 1987.

The star-like object on the right of the picture below is *supernova* 1987A. It became visible in the southern hemisphere in February 1987.

Glossary ....

This glossary explains some of the words you might come across while reading about astronomy. Words in *italic type* have their own entry elsewhere in the glossary.

asterism A pattern of stars that is part of a *constellation*. The Plough (Big Dipper) is an asterism.

asteroid A large piece of metal or rock and metal that orbits the Sun.

atmosphere The layers of gases that surround a planet or a star.

aurora Shimmering lights in the night sky caused by an interaction between the Earth's *atmosphere* and the *solar wind*. They appear near the Earth's north and south poles.

cluster A group of stars or galaxies that are relatively close together.

constellation A group of stars that seems to form a pattern in the night sky.

corona The outer, hottest part of the Sun's *atmosphere*.

elongation The position a planet is in when it appears farthest to the east or west of the Sun.

light year The distance light travels in one year: 9.46 million million* km (5.8 million million miles). Distances in space are measured in light years.

magnitude The scale used to measure how bright things are in the night sky.

mare (plural: maria) An area on the Moon that was once flooded with molten rock which later cooled and hardened.

meteor A *meteoroid* that burns up as it enters Earth's *atmosphere*.

meteorite A *meteoroid* that has landed on the Earth's surface.

meteoroid A small piece of dust or rock in space.

opposition The position a planet is in when it appears opposite the Sun, and Earth is between that planet and the Sun.

orbit The path taken by an object in space, such as a moon or planet, as it goes around another object, such as a planet or star.

reflector telescope A type of telescope that uses mirrors and lenses to make things look bigger.

refractor telescope A type of telescope that uses lenses alone to make things look bigger.

solar wind A constant stream of invisible particles which the Sun blows out into space.

sunspot A dark area on the Sun's surface where it is cooler than elsewhere on the Sun.

supernova An exploding star.

universe Space and everything that exists in it.

*US = trillion

Index .....

Page numbers in *italics* show where to find pictures. Where there are several pages for a particular entry, numbers in **bold** tell you where to find the main explanation.

Acknowledgements

Every effort has been made to trace the copyright holders of the material in this book. If any rights have been omitted, the publishers offer to rectify this in any subsequent editions following notification. The publishers are grateful to the following organizations and individuals for their permission to reproduce material (t=top, m=middle, b=bottom, l=left, r=right):

Cover (l) © Digital Vision, (m) NASA, (mr) © CORBIS, (br) NASA; **p1** © Fred Espenak/Science Photo Library; **p2–3** © Dr. Seth Shostak/Science Photo Library; **p4** © Larry Landolfi/Science Photo Library; **p4** (m) © Royal Observatory, Edinburgh/AAO/Science Photo Library; **p5** (tr) © Jean-Charles Cuillandre/Canada-France-Hawaii Telescope/Science Photo Library; **p6–7** © Dr. Fred Espenak/Science Photo Library; **p12–13** © Jean Miele/CORBIS; **p13** (tl) © Simon Fraser/Science Photo Library, (mr) © Space Telescope Science Institute/NASA/Science Photo Library; **p14–15** NASA; **p15** © Scharmer et al/Royal Swedish Academy of Sciences/Science Photo Library; **p16–17** Courtesy of NASA/JPL/Caltec; **p16** (ml) © Digital Vision; **p17** (tr) NASA; **p18** (tr) © Rev. Ronald Royer/Science Photo Library; **p19** (tr) © Kenneth W. Fink/Science Photo Library, (bl) © Dan Schechter/Science Photo Library; **p20** © Celestial Image Company/Science Photo Library; **p21** © Celestial Image Company/Science Photo Library; **p22** (tl) © European Southern Observatory/Science Photo Library; **p23** (tr) © Allan Morton/Dennis Milon/Science Photo Library, (bl) STScI/NASA; **p24** © Eckhard Slawik/Science Photo Library; **p25** (tr) © John Sanford/Science Photo Library, (ml) © Roger Ressmeyer/CORBIS; **p36** (tl) © Chris Butler/Science Photo Library, (mr) © US Geological Survey/Science Photo Library, (br) © Fred Espenak/Science Photo Library; **p37** (tr) NASA, (br) NASA; **p38** NASA; **p39** NASA; **p40** NASA; **p41** © CORBIS; **p42** (b) © Tony & Daphne Hallas/Science Photo Library; **p43** © Jerry Lodriguss/Science Photo Library; **p44–45** © Michael Giannechini/Science Photo Library; **p44** © Royal Observatory, Edinburgh/Science Photo Library; **p45** © Royal Observatory, Edinburgh/Science Photo Library

Image in fact boxes used with kind permission from Orion Telescopes and Binoculars: © 2003 Orion Telescopes & Binoculars

Managing designer: Mary Cartwright.
Cover designed by Nelupa Hussain.
Photographic manipulation by Emma Julings and John Russell.

With many thanks to Alice Pearcey.

Internet links

Throughout this book, we have recommended interesting websites where you can find out more about astronomy. To visit the recommended sites, go to the **Usborne Quicklinks Website** at **www.usborne-quicklinks.com** and type the keywords "discovery astronomy". There you will find links to click on to take you to all the sites. Here are some of the things you can do on the recommended sites:

- Take a virtual tour of the Sun.

- See amazing pictures taken by some of the world's largest telescopes.

At Usborne Quicklinks, you will also find an astronomy pronunciation guide with links to click on to hear how to say the names of stars, galaxies and other things in space.

Internet safety

When using the Internet, please make sure you follow these guidelines:

- Ask your parent's or guardian's permission before you connect to the Internet.

- When you are on the Internet, never tell anyone your full name, address or telephone number, and ask an adult before you give your email address.

- If a website asks you to log in or register by typing your name or email address, ask an adult's permission first.

- If you do receive an email from someone you don't know, tell an adult and do not reply to the email.

Computer not essential
If you don't have access to the Internet, don't worry. This book is a complete, superb, self-contained reference book on its own.

Site availability

The links in Usborne Quicklinks are regularly reviewed and updated, but occasionally you may get a message that a site is unavailable. This might be temporary, so try again later, or even the next day. If any of the sites closes down, we will, if possible, replace it with a suitable alternative, so you will always find an up-to-date list of sites in Usborne Quicklinks.

What you need

Most websites listed in this book can be accessed using a standard home computer and a web browser (the software that lets you look at information from the Internet). Some sites need extra programs (plug-ins) to play sound or show videos or animations. If you go to a site and do not have the necessary plug-in, a message will come up on the screen. There is usually a button on the site that you can click on to download the plug-in. Alternatively, go to **Usborne Quicklinks** and click on "Net Help". There, you can find links to download plug-ins.

Notes for parents and guardians

The websites described in this book are regularly reviewed and the links in Usborne Quicklinks are updated. However, the content of a website may change at any time and Usborne Publishing is not responsible for the content on any website other than its own.

We recommend that children are supervised while on the Internet, that they do not use Internet chat rooms, and that you use Internet filtering software to block unsuitable material. Please ensure that your children read and follow the safety guidelines printed on the left. For more information, see the "Net Help" area on the Usborne Quicklinks Website.